MCCARTHYISM

The Red Scare

by Brian Fitzgerald

McCarthyism

The Red Scare

by Brian Fitzgerald

Content Adviser: Derek Shouba, Adjunct History Professor
and Assistant Provost, Roosevelt University

Reading Adviser: Katie Van Sluys, Ph.D.,
School of Education, DePaul University

COMPASS POINT BOOKS
MINNEAPOLIS, MINNESOTA

COMPASS POINT BOOKS

3109 West 50th Street, #115
Minneapolis, MN 55410

Visit Compass Point Books on the Internet at
www.compasspointbooks.com
or e-mail your request to
custserv@compasspointbooks.com

For Compass Point Books
Jennifer VanVoorst, Jaime Martens, XNR Productions, Inc.,
Catherine Neitge, Keith Griffin, and Carol Jones

Produced by White-Thomson Publishing Ltd.

For White-Thomson Publishing
Stephen White-Thomson, Susan Crean, Amy Sparks,
Tinstar Design Ltd., Derek Shouba, Justine Dunn, Laurel Haines,
and Timothy Griffin

Library of Congress Cataloging-in-Publication Data
Fitzgerald, Brian. 1972–
  McCarthyism : the red scare / by Brian Fitzgerald.
     p. cm. — (Snapshots in history)
  Includes bibliographical references and index.

  ISBN-13: 978-0-7565-2007-6 (hardcover)

  ISBN-10: 0-7565-2007-X (hardcover)

  1. McCarthy, Joseph, 1908–1957—Juvenile literature. 2. Anticommunist movements—United States—History—20th century—
Juvenile literature. 3. Legislators—United States—Biography—Juvenile
literature. 4. United States. Congress. Senate—Biography–Juvenile
literature. 5. Cold War—Juvenile literature. I. Title. II. Series.
  E743.5.F48 2007
  973.921—dc22   2006003005

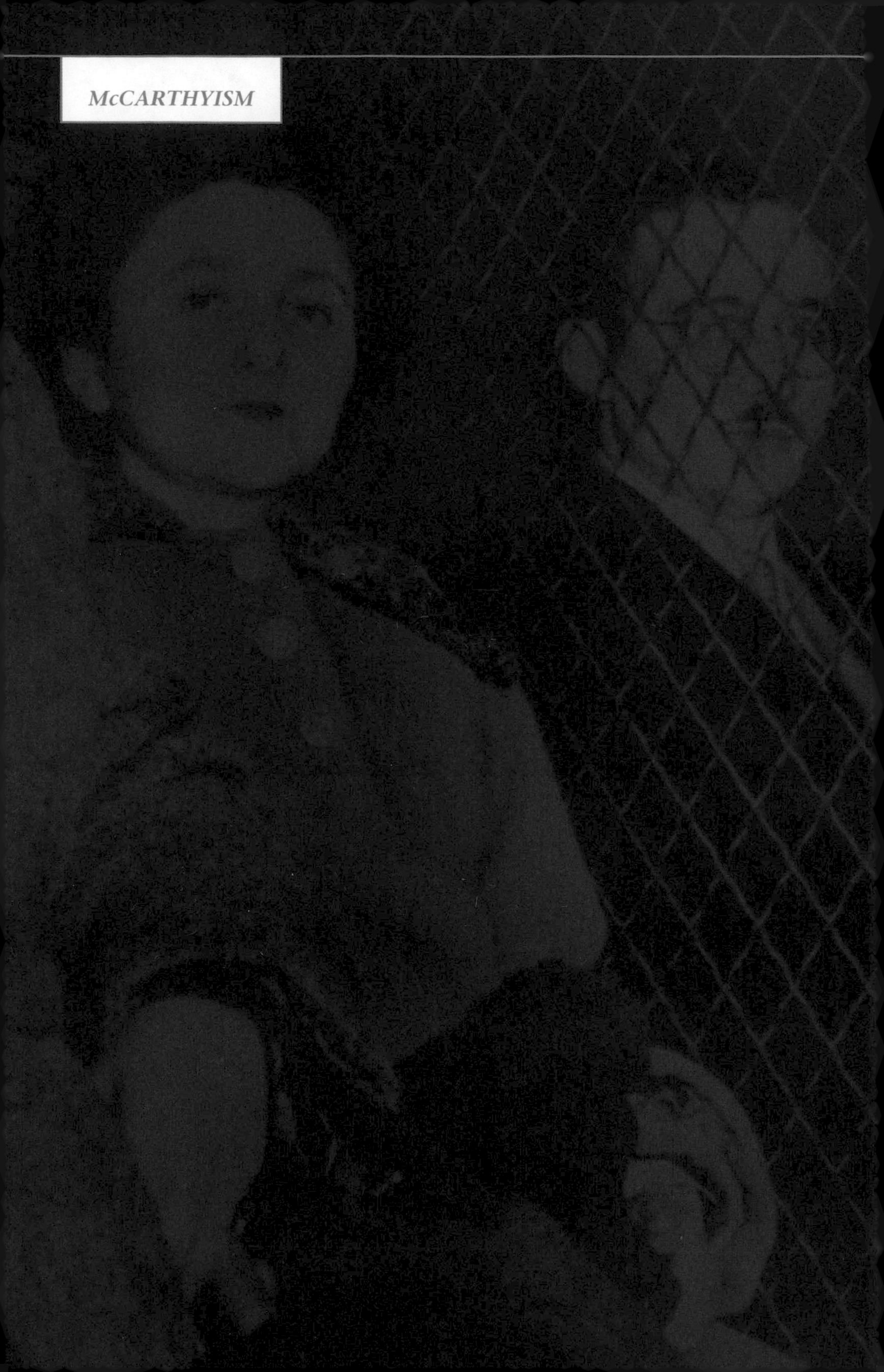

CONTENTS

Red Alert 8

The Rise of Communism 16

The Cold War and Containment 28

McCarthy Grabs the Spotlight 38

The Atomic Age 50

The McCarthy Committee 60

The Fall of McCarthy...72

Aftermath and Lessons 80

Timeline 86

On the Web..89

Glossary...90

Source Notes...91

Select Bibliography...93

Index 94

About the Author/Image Credits 96

Red Alert

In February 1950, a husky United States senator from Wisconsin named Joseph McCarthy set out on a speaking tour that would take him across the country. The speeches he gave were part of an annual Republican tradition in honor of Abraham Lincoln's birthday. McCarthy's first stop was in the small town of Wheeling, West Virginia, on February 9. Few in the crowd of about 275 people knew much about the senator. The 41-year-old McCarthy had done little to make himself known since he was elected to the U.S. Senate in 1946. But this changed with the speech he gave on that cold evening.

McCarthy's speech focused on the troubled relationship between the United States and its main enemy, the Soviet Union. At the time, many Americans feared the spread of communism, the

Soviet form of government. In the communist system, the state controls all land and business. The Soviet government also limited other rights of its people. The government owned all the newspapers and radio and TV stations and also punished people for their religious beliefs. This went against the values of most Americans, who saw the freedoms to worship, own land, and voice their opinions as basic rights of all people.

Senator Joseph McCarthy was the main figure in the anticommunist effort of the early 1950s.

During his speech, McCarthy warned that Americans were losing the power struggle against the Soviets. In the five years since the end of World War II, communists had risen to power in China and several nations in Eastern Europe. McCarthy claimed that traitors within the U.S. government were aiding the spread of communism.

In dramatic fashion, McCarthy held up a piece of paper and reportedly spoke these words:

> *I have here in my hand a list of 205 [men] that were known to the secretary of state as being members of the Communist Party and who, nevertheless, are still working and shaping the policy of the State Department.*

This was a serious charge. The State Department is the part of the U.S. government that sets foreign policy. Communists working in such an important area could influence how the United States dealt with the Soviet Union. Using that influence, they could weaken the fight against communism worldwide. They also could be working as spies, giving the Soviets top-secret government information about atomic weapons and other areas of U.S. military and political strategy.

MUTUAL MISTRUST

Spying, also known as espionage, is the practice of obtaining military or political secrets from a rival. After World War II, both the United States and the Soviet Union used secret agents to spy on one another. The fear of communist spies in the U.S. government was one of the main causes for the popularity of McCarthy's ideas.

Just as scary as the threat of communists in government was McCarthy's claim that Dean Acheson, the U.S. secretary of state at the time, knew about them. If President Harry S. Truman and his top aides could not keep communists out of the highest levels of government, some Americans worried, how could they defeat them around the world?

No one saw McCarthy's list naming communists in the government, but it made the national news.

11

The details of McCarthy's speech were not widely reported in newspapers the following day. However, as the senator continued to make similar claims along his speaking tour, the news media in the United States began to take greater notice. Without showing anyone his list or naming a single offender, McCarthy was grabbing headlines across the country.

Before this series of speeches, McCarthy had been a minor player in U.S. politics. He was unknown to most Americans outside of his home state of Wisconsin. By seizing upon the public fear of communism, McCarthy soon became the central figure in the movement to hunt down communists.

The United States was already in a period of intense anticommunism that came to be called the Red Scare. It is referred to this way because the color red is often associated with communism. Red was also the main color of the Soviet flag.

The hysteria of the Red Scare made it easy for the public to believe McCarthy's charges—even though he offered no real proof. Even so, the tireless search for communists that McCarthy and others led would trample upon the basic rights of many of the Americans they accused—rights that are clearly outlined in the U.S. Constitution's Bill of Rights. Though being a communist is not a crime, many people lost their jobs, served prison time, or had their lives shattered as a result of McCarthy's accusations.

During the Red Scare, public rallies to protest communists in government, schools, and other institutions were common.

THE FIRST AMENDMENT

Shortly after the U.S. Constitution was drawn up in 1789, the writers added 10 amendments to it, known as the Bill of Rights. These amendments were designed to protect individuals from the power of the government. The First Amendment protects the right of free speech. This includes the right to speak out against the U.S. government or support ideas that are unpopular—including communism.

Anticommunist government hearings drew huge coverage in newspapers and on radio and television.

McCarthy was not the only politician of the period whose questionable tactics ruined lives and careers. But he is the one most closely associated with this sad and strange chapter in American history, which is often called the McCarthy era. The senator's practice of accusing others without hard evidence became known as McCarthyism. ◥

The Rise of Communism

Chapter

2

The anticommunist hysteria of the early 1950s was actually the second Red Scare in the United States. The first occurred after a revolution in Russia in October 1917. At the time, the Soviet Union did not yet exist, and Russia was an independent country. Millions of Russian peasants were living in severe poverty. Starvation was a common cause of death. A group of communists called Bolsheviks promised to take property from the rich and divide it equally among all workers. This appealed to many of Russia's people. Many in the lower classes saw the communist system as the only way to feed their families. The Revolution of 1917 brought the communist Bolsheviks into power in Russia.

But the Bolsheviks were also brutal rulers who jailed or murdered anyone who opposed them.

There were no elections, so regular citizens had no voice in government. The Russian people lost the few freedoms they had, including the right to worship freely. For many poor farmers, conditions were worse than ever. They had to give up their crops to the government and were left without enough food to feed their families.

During the Revolution of 1917, Bolshevik troops overthrew the Russian government based in Petrograd, which is today known as St. Petersburg.

Many Americans were horrified by this harsh new system of government, in which free speech and religion seemed to have no place. More troubling was the communist call for a worldwide revolution of the working classes. To many, it appeared as though such a revolution was beginning to take shape in the United States in 1919.

During the 1920s, union workers across the country — including bakers in New York — went on strike to win better working conditions.

During that year, more than 4 million union workers around the United States went on strike. Most strikers were honest workers who wanted better pay, safer working conditions, or shorter workdays. But many Americans worried that communists or radicals who wanted to overthrow the government caused the strikes.

19

This fear increased after a radical plot to send mail bombs to government officials and leaders of large companies was uncovered in late April 1919. In early June of that year, a bomb exploded outside the home of U.S. Attorney General A. Mitchell Palmer. It killed the man who carried it. To many people, this was a clear sign that radicals wanted to start a revolution in America.

That summer, Palmer named 24-year-old J. Edgar Hoover the head of the new General Intelligence Division at the Justice Department. Hoover's main task was to find and prosecute radicals. His first major raid rounded up hundreds of Russian immigrants who were suspected radicals. Nearly 250 of them were deported back to their homeland. Many of the deportees had not done anything wrong. Their only crime was belonging to an organization that was viewed as radical. Still, the raid won praise, and Hoover and the attorney general were hailed as heroes.

The government soon turned its sights to the two separate communist parties that had recently formed in the United States. The Bolshevik

THE CPUSA

In 1921, the two communist parties in the United States joined together to form the Communist Party of the United States (CPUSA). The CPUSA later operated under the control of the Soviet Union. Formed in 1922, this new nation was made up of Russia and several bordering republics. One of the CPUSA's main goals was to recruit spies within the U.S. government who could report back to the Soviet Union.

leaders in Russia believed that communism could not succeed unless it gained support in other nations. One of their main targets was the United States. Both the new parties, the Communist Party of America and the Communist Labor Party, pledged to uphold the philosophy of the Bolsheviks in Russia.

J. Edgar Hoover became the director of the Bureau of Investigations, which later became the Federal Bureau of Investigation (FBI). Appointed in 1924, he held the position for nearly 50 years.

Thousands of suspected communists were arrested in the early 1920 Palmer Raids, named after the attorney general. Suspects were denied many of the basic rights of the accused. They were not allowed to speak to a lawyer or even contact their families. Bail was set so high that it was impossible to meet. Some people were held for months, even though they were never charged with a crime. Most of the cases were thrown out due to a lack of real evidence.

The first Red Scare fizzled out in the mid-1920s, as people realized the communist threat was not as bad as they had feared. But with the next decade came difficult times that made some Americans reconsider the possible benefits of communism.

The Great Depression of the 1930s was the greatest economic crisis in U.S. history. During its peak, one in four workers was unemployed. As banks were forced to close, many Americans saw their life savings disappear. Millions struggled to feed and clothe their families. Worse yet, the government seemed powerless to stop the downward spiral.

Scenes of unemployed men lined up outside soup kitchens were typical during the Great Depression.

Many viewed the Great Depression as a failure of capitalism. Some Americans looked to other economic models as possible answers for the country's troubles. Many workers and intellectuals alike were attracted to communism, which seemed to guarantee a comfortable way of life for all people.

The Communist Party of the United States (CPUSA) took up the cause of the unemployed and union workers. CPUSA members played important roles in several large labor unions. They helped plan strikes and rallies in an effort to gain better pay and working conditions for union members.

COMMUNISTS FOR CIVIL RIGHTS

Many African-Americans and supporters of civil rights were drawn to the CPUSA because of its platform of racial equality. Black and white party members worked side-by-side as equals, which was not the case in most of American society. The party actively fought segregation and unfair treatment in the workplace. In 1932, the party even ran James Ford as its vice president, the first black man to run in a U.S. presidential election. The Communist Party's fight for equality made it even more unpopular among opponents who were also against integration.

Communists also supported the new government programs introduced by President Franklin Delano Roosevelt (FDR). Elected in 1932, Roosevelt, a Democrat, created a number of government programs that sought to bring the nation out of the Great Depression. His plan, known as the New Deal, brought relief to the poor by providing jobs and financial aid. Roosevelt also believed these programs would help boost the morale of the victims of the Great Depression. But not everyone supported his programs. Many conservatives, especially Republican members of Congress, did not think the government should play such a big role in shaping the economy.

President Franklin D. Roosevelt (seated, at right) met with some of the workers who found jobs as part of his New Deal.

25

By the late 1930s, membership in CPUSA grew to nearly 70,000. Thousands more Americans were not official members of CPUSA but still supported communist ideals. This represented only a small fraction of the U.S. population, but some members of the government still saw the influence of communists as a big threat. In 1937, Martin Dies, a Republican member of Congress from Texas, was chosen to head the Special House Committee on Un-American Activities, later called HUAC. This committee was set up to investigate the promotion of un-American ideas. Many of HUAC's conservative members were opposed to the New Deal and equated many of its programs with communism. As one HUAC member said:

> *It seems to me that the New Deal is working hand in glove with the Communist Party.*

At that time, Dies and his committee used many of the tactics later made popular by Joseph McCarthy. They bullied witnesses and made charges without evidence to back up their statements. Any organizations that HUAC did not support were branded as un-American, as were any witnesses who did not cooperate.

The negative views toward communists at home and abroad soon changed drastically. During World War II, the United States and the Soviet Union put aside their differences to fight a common enemy, Nazi Germany.

American communists who had helped organize labor strikes were calling for workers to work longer and harder to support the war effort. Americans grew to respect their Soviet allies, who fought bravely in terrible conditions to drive the Nazis out of their homeland. During the war, the United States sent more than $11 billion in aid to the Soviets. But the goodwill created during the war would not last. ◣

Soviets troops guarded German prisoners during World War II. The Soviets battled against the Germans and gained the support of the United States and its allies.

The Cold War and Containment

With victory over the Germans within their grasp, the three leaders of the Allied nations of World War II held a historic conference. It took place in the Soviet resort town of Yalta in February 1945. U.S. President Franklin Roosevelt, British Prime Minister Winston Churchill, and Soviet Premier Joseph Stalin met to discuss plans for postwar Europe.

The three leaders agreed that after the war, Germany would be split into four zones. The United States, Great Britain, the Soviet Union, and France would each occupy one of the zones. They also decided that Berlin, the German capital city that was in the Soviet-controlled zone, would also be divided into four sections.

Roosevelt and Churchill realized that they could not have defeated Germany without the help of the Soviets. But they wanted to limit the communist influence in Europe. Both leaders called for elections in areas freed from the Germans. This included Poland and other Eastern European countries occupied by the Soviets. Stalin agreed to these terms, but no plans were made for when the elections would take place.

Winston Churchill (left), Franklin Roosevelt, and Joseph Stalin met at Yalta to plot the future of Europe after World War II.

On April 12, 1945, Roosevelt died unexpectedly, and Vice President Harry S. Truman became the U.S. president. Within a few months, Truman gave the order to use atomic weapons for the first time in history. Just days after U.S. planes dropped atomic bombs on the Japanese cities of Hiroshima and Nagasaki, World War II was over.

Soon after the end of World War II, tensions began to mount between the Soviet Union and the United States. Stalin broke the agreement he had made in Yalta to hold free elections in the Soviet-occupied states. Instead, he installed communist governments in several Eastern European countries, including Poland. This was the beginning of the Cold War between the United States and the Soviet Union. This long rivalry between the world's two most powerful nations would last into the 1990s.

In March 1947, Truman introduced a policy to contain, or limit, the expansion of communism to other countries. The so-called Truman Doctrine pledged aid to free governments around the globe in their fight against communism. This new strategy became known as containment.

Three months later, U.S. Secretary of State George Marshall announced another aggressive plan. The European Recovery Act, or Marshall Plan, would rebuild areas of Europe that had been devastated during World War II. U.S. leaders knew that communism often gained support in nations

President Harry S. Truman shaped U.S. policy toward communism at home and overseas during the first years of the Cold War.

with economic troubles. They hoped that boosting the economies of European nations would prevent the spread of communism in those areas.

The Marshall Plan was a success. Over the next four years, the United States sent nearly $13 billion in aid to 16 noncommunist European nations. The shipments of fuel, food, machinery, and other materials helped these nations get back on their feet. The threat of communism in those areas soon quieted down.

31

Meanwhile, the Soviets took aggressive steps to expand the communist influence in Europe. The first great "battle" of the Cold War took place in the divided German capital of Berlin. In June 1948, the Soviet army blocked the roads and railways that led to the areas of the city occupied by the Allies, known as West Berlin. This meant that the 2 million people living in West Berlin could not receive any food, medicine, or other vital materials from the outside. In response, British and U.S. cargo planes began flying around the clock to

Cargo planes brought much-needed supplies to the people of West Berlin during the Berlin Airlift.

bring supplies into West Berlin. The operation, known as the Berlin Airlift, lasted 10 months. The United States had not backed down to the Soviet Union, which ended the blockade in May 1949.

Besides dealing with communism abroad, President Truman was also under political pressure to tackle communism at home. He heard constant rumblings from Republicans about communists or communist sympathizers working in the U.S. government. Truman was up for reelection in 1948 and wanted to shed the label of being "soft" on communism.

One week after proposing the Truman Doctrine, the president signed Executive Order 9835. This order called for an investigation into the loyalty of all federal employees. Any employees suspected of disloyalty were brought before a loyalty board. Suspects were not told the names of their accusers and were not allowed to review the charges against them. This made it difficult for the accused to mount a proper defense. Despite the problems with this system of investigation, it seemed to prove that relatively few communists were working in the U.S. government. Over the next five and a half years, the FBI reviewed files of 4.7 million federal employees and applicants. Only 560 of these people were dismissed or denied a job. No cases of people spying were found. State and local governments and private institutions such as universities soon adopted similar loyalty programs.

Truman hoped the loyalty program would silence his critics and make the question of communists in government disappear. Unfortunately, a high-profile scandal would undo most of his efforts and convince many Americans that communists were playing a key role in the U.S. government.

In July 1948, Whittaker Chambers, a former communist spy, testified before the Special House Committee on Un-American Activities (HUAC). Chambers claimed to have been part of a Soviet spy network in the U.S. government during the 1930s. Among the other spies he identified was a former State Department official named Alger Hiss. From 1933 to 1946, Hiss had held several key positions in the government. He attended the historic Yalta Conference in 1945 and served as the secretary general of the conference that created the United Nations.

Hiss appeared before HUAC to dispute Chambers' charges. He claimed that he had never met Chambers and later called him "a self-confessed liar, spy, and

THE SMITH ACT

In 1948, the Truman administration went after CPUSA itself. Party leaders were charged with violating the Smith Act of 1940, which made it illegal for anyone to belong to a group that wanted to overthrow the government. Eleven leaders of CPUSA were found guilty and sentenced to three to five years in prison. They were not convicted of any overt acts to overthrow the government—belonging to CPUSA was enough. The trial did serious damage to the party by taking away its top leaders, and their legal defense drained much of the party's funds. Although this was a major victory for the anticommunists, it did not do much to calm concerns about communism in America.

traitor." A graduate of Harvard Law School, Hiss was well-spoken and well-dressed. Many top officials voiced support for him, including Truman and Secretary of State Acheson. Most HUAC members wanted to drop the case against Hiss due to a lack of hard evidence.

Alger Hiss testified before HUAC in August 1948.

35

But one member of the committee, California Congressman (and future U.S. president) Richard Nixon, insisted on pursuing the case further. After meeting with Chambers privately, Nixon was convinced that Hiss was not telling the truth. In November, Chambers led HUAC investigators to a pumpkin patch in Maryland. He produced five rolls of microfilm that were hidden in a hollowed-out pumpkin. It seemed like a storyline out of a spy novel. Chambers claimed the "pumpkin papers" were secret government documents given to him by Hiss. He also turned over 65 pages of typed copies of State Department files that he said he received from Hiss.

THE HOLLYWOOD TEN

During the late 1940s, HUAC took aim at communists in Hollywood. In October 1947, a group of 10 screenwriters and directors were called before the committee to answer questions about their beliefs. All 10 refused to cooperate, citing their First Amendment right to free speech. Every one of them was charged with contempt of Congress and sent to prison. The heads of the film industry vowed not to hire any of the "Hollywood Ten" unless they swore they were not communists. This was the start of the blacklist, which prevented many actors, directors, and writers from working in Hollywood during the late 1940s and 1950s because they were accused of being communists.

The pumpkin papers were key pieces of evidence in the case against Hiss, who claimed they were forgeries. In January 1950, Hiss was convicted of perjury for lying under oath about

his communist connections. He served nearly four years in prison, all the time insisting that he was innocent.

Members of the "Hollywood Ten" and their lawyers appeared outside the courthouse where they were sentenced for contempt of Congress.

For many, the Hiss case proved that communists were working behind the scenes to topple the U.S. government. Some were convinced that Hiss could not have risen to such a high level in government without help from other communists. Anticommunism in the United States was soaring. Just three weeks after Hiss was convicted, Joseph McCarthy would fuel the hysteria with his memorable speech in Wheeling, West Virginia.

McCarthy Grabs the Spotlight

In many ways, Joseph McCarthy embodied the American dream. He overcame a poor childhood and became successful through hard work and a good education. McCarthy was born on November 14, 1908. He was the fourth of seven children of Irish-American parents who owned a farm in Grand Chute, Wisconsin. As a boy, Joseph went to a school where students in all eight grades studied in a single classroom. He left school after the eighth grade to work on the family farm. He later started his own business raising chickens and worked as a manager of a grocery store.

At age 20, McCarthy realized that he would not get far without an education. He decided to go to high school. He understood the value of hard work and completed the entire four-year course in a single school year. McCarthy went on to attend Marquette University and graduated with a law degree in 1935. He started his own law firm and also became interested in politics. A Democrat, he was a big supporter of FDR and the New Deal.

Joseph McCarthy graduated from high school in 1930.

McCarthy created the image of "Tail-Gunner Joe" to help win support of voters when he ran for the U.S. Senate.

In 1939, McCarthy was elected circuit judge, which meant he would preside over cases in the three counties in his district in Wisconsin. He also switched political parties and became a Republican. After the Japanese attacked the U.S. naval base at Pearl Harbor, Hawaii, on December 7, 1941, young men were drafted into military service. As a judge, McCarthy was exempt from being drafted. But in June 1942, the 33-year-old judge took a leave of absence to join the Marines. He was assigned to a Marine bomber squadron that saw combat against the Japanese.

TAIL-GUNNER JOE

McCarthy often exaggerated his war record to help his political career. For example, he was photographed in the rear seat, or tail-gun position, of a dive bomber and called himself "Tail-Gunner Joe," which led voters to believe he had fought bravely in combat. In fact, most of his work had been behind a desk. He did tag along for a handful of missions but was never in any real danger. The number of missions he claimed to have taken part in seemed to increase every few years. He also hid the fact that the "war wound" he sometimes boasted about was a broken foot he suffered when he slipped off a ladder at a party on a Navy ship.

While still stationed in the Pacific, McCarthy ran for the U.S. Senate in 1944—and lost. Two years later, he decided to run again and won after campaigning tirelessly throughout the state of Wisconsin.

McCarthy failed to make a major impression during his first three years as a senator. He hoped to make a name for himself by joining the crusade against communism. But even he could not have guessed the impact his Wheeling speech on February 9, 1950, would soon have.

McCarthy's charge that hundreds of Communists held jobs in the U.S. government shocked the nation. But almost immediately after the speech, McCarthy changed his claim that 205 communists worked in the State Department. In Denver, Colorado, the second stop on his speaking tour, he told reporters he had a list of 207 people considered to be "bad risks." When reporters asked to see the list, McCarthy said he left it in his other suit, which was still on the plane. In fact, McCarthy did not have any list. He was basing his claims on a letter that had been written more than three years earlier.

The letter he was referring to discussed 3,000 people who were being transferred to the State Department at the end of World War II. A screening board had recommended that 284 of these people not be given permanent jobs. As it turns out, 79 of the 284 ended up leaving before the screening process was finished. Senator McCarthy got his 205 figure by subtracting 79 from 284. In a radio interview in Salt Lake City, Utah, on February 10, McCarthy reduced his charge to 57 card-carrying

BASELESS SOURCES

The problem with McCarthy referring to the State Department letter was that the original letter never actually mentioned communism. It only stated that the employees were not being recommended for jobs. McCarthy had no way of knowing if the 205 employees still worked for the government or how many had been cleared in the years in between. He did not know a single one of their names or why they were not being recommended in the first place.

communists in the State Department. He used the same figure the following day in Reno, Nevada. He later claimed that this was the number he had used in Wheeling, rather than 205. He also sent an angry letter to President Truman, demanding that he order Secretary of State Acheson to give the names of "disloyal" employees working in the State Department.

Truman was furious. He told reporters there was not a word of truth in McCarthy's accusations. He said that by seeking to damage his own government, McCarthy was actually helping the Soviet Union. State Department officials denied all charges and demanded to see McCarthy's list.

Newspapers continued to cover the story, even though McCarthy could not back up his claims. His sensational charges made for good headlines. Because of McCarthy's powerful position and the seriousness of the charges, most reporters assumed he was telling the truth. Even newspapers that questioned his tactics put McCarthy on the front page. As one newspaper editorial explained:

> *It is unbelievable that a United States senator would publicly and repeatedly make such charges if he did not have any evidence to support them.*

But McCarthy was not just taking up a battle against communism. He was also creating a political battle between Republicans and Democrats.

43

The Alger Hiss case had done serious political damage to the Democrats. McCarthy's wild charges ensured that the issue of communists working within the government remained in the spotlight. Democrats believed McCarthy continued to make accusations solely for this reason. Republicans approved of his methods because they showed the Democratic Truman administration in a bad light. In some ways, both parties were more concerned with making the other look bad than actually uncovering the truth.

On February 20, 1950, McCarthy presented his case before the Senate. By this time, he claimed he had 81 names. Most of his files were at least two years old, but he tried to pass them off as new information. Many of the cases were held over from a 1948 Senate subcommittee hearing on the loyalty program. As McCarthy tried to present his case, his opponents in the Senate constantly interrupted him. They wanted the senator to name the card-carrying communists, but he refused. McCarthy said it would be unfair to give their names since they had not been charged with a crime. His critics were tired of his stall tactics. In less than two weeks, McCarthy had changed his accusations several times. Now he was dodging questions and giving few hard facts. To some, this was proof that his charges had no merit. The proceedings dragged on for six hours. In the end, the Senate was left with more questions than answers.

In March 1950, a Senate subcommittee, often referred to as the Tydings Committee, began hearings to investigate charges about people who were security risks working in the State Department. The chairman, Millard Tydings, a Democrat from Maryland, used the hearings to attack McCarthy.

When pressed for names, McCarthy finally gave the names of nine people. Each of the accused was called in to answer the charges, and each time, McCarthy's case against them quickly fell apart. As soon as one case was disproved, McCarthy moved on to the next.

In his appearance before the Tydings Committee in March 1950, McCarthy presented nine cases of suspected communists working in the State Department.

McCarthy created the biggest stir when he promised to uncover "the top Russian espionage agent" during the hearings—a man named Owen Lattimore. McCarthy was so confident that he told reporters:

> *I am willing to stand or fall on this one. If I am shown to be wrong on this, I think the subcommittee would be justified in not taking my other cases too seriously.*

McCarthy's case took a major hit when J. Edgar Hoover said that the FBI had no proof that Lattimore was a communist. In his typical fashion, McCarthy quickly backed off of his original statement. He now called Lattimore the "architect" of U.S. foreign policy in the Far East. In fact, Lattimore had not worked for the State Department since the mid-1940s, and even then, it was only in a limited role.

RED CHINA

In October 1949, the People's Republic of China was formed. Its communist government led by Mao Tse-tung had won a long, bloody civil war over the nationalist forces of Chiang Kai-shek, who had been supported by the United States. This news only added to the Red Scare in the United States. Now two of the biggest countries in the world—China and the Soviet Union—had communist governments.

McCarthy called in Louis Budenz, a former communist, to identify Lattimore as a party member. Budenz had been a key witness in the trials of the 11 CPUSA leaders and had also testified against Alger Hiss. Oddly enough, Budenz had given the FBI thousands of hours of testimony since leaving the party in 1945, but he had never mentioned Lattimore until a few days before appearing before this committee. Although Budenz's testimony cast some doubt on Lattimore, there was no real proof he was a communist. And he clearly was not a top Soviet spy.

As the hearings entered their third month, patience among the committee members began to wear thin. McCarthy had made plenty of allegations,

In the early 1950s, many Americans feared the spread of communism around the world.

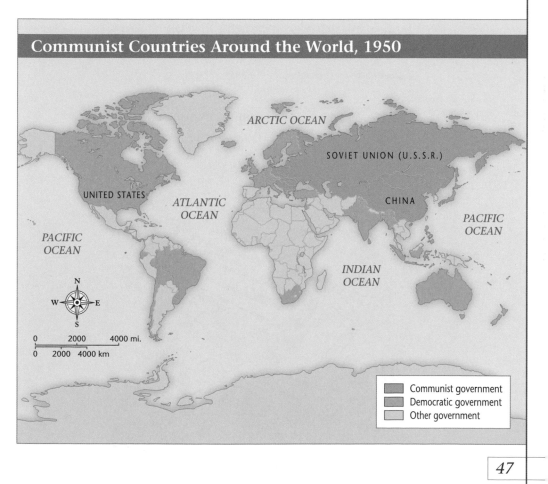

Communist Countries Around the World, 1950

ARCTIC OCEAN

SOVIET UNION (U.S.S.R.)

UNITED STATES

ATLANTIC OCEAN

CHINA

PACIFIC OCEAN

PACIFIC OCEAN

INDIAN OCEAN

N
W   E
S

0   2000   4000 mi.
0   2000   4000 km

Communist government
Democratic government
Other government

but he had yet to expose a single communist. During a shouting match with McCarthy, Senator Scott Lucas of Illinois demanded:

> *The time has come to call a spade a spade ... not a shred of evidence has been presented— not a shred.*

The hearings concluded at the end of June 1950. The Tydings Committee issued a report that criticized McCarthy and his tactics. McCarthy had accomplished little during the hearings, but national polls showed that the majority of Americans supported his cause.

Herb Block was a cartoonist for The Washington Post *who often criticized the tactics of McCarthy and HUAC. In one cartoon, Herblock, as he was known, implied that red-hunting politicians didn't care who they ran over in their search for communists.*

There is little doubt that McCarthy's growing popularity was aided by global events. For example, on June 25, 1950, communist troops from North Korea poured into South Korea in an effort to overthrow its democratic government. Within days, U.S. troops were rushed into South Korea, but they were beaten back. To some, it appeared as if the U.S. government was powerless to stop the spread of communism.

FIGHTING JOE

One of McCarthy's biggest critics was columnist Drew Pearson. In December 1950, the two were seated at the same table at a fancy dinner dance. Early in the evening, the two traded insults and nearly came to blows. As Pearson was leaving the party, McCarthy grabbed him from behind, spun him around and kicked him. Richard Nixon jumped in to break up the fight.

By this time, McCarthy was receiving 25,000 letters of support each day. People from across the country sent money to aid his search. Some people even sent information on suspected communists. The era of McCarthyism was well under way. ◣

The Atomic Age

The heightened fear during the Red Scare had become more intense after Americans learned of a new threat: nuclear war. The entire nation was shocked when the Soviet Union successfully tested its first nuclear bomb in August 1949. Until then, the United States was the only country that had atomic weapons. The world had seen the atomic bomb's devastating effects when the United States dropped two of them on Hiroshima and Nagasaki, Japan, near the end of World War II. Now, the Soviet Union had the power to wipe out entire U.S. cities with the push of a button.

Americans grew more worried about the Soviet nuclear threat. They reasoned that the Soviets could not have built an atomic bomb without help from spies.

The makers of bomb shelters claimed that they could protect a family from a hydrogen bomb blast only three miles (five kilometers) away.

During the McCarthy era, many people believed that a nuclear war was unavoidable. School children prepared for an attack with duck-and-cover drills. When an alarm sounded, they dropped to the floor and covered their heads. People built bomb shelters in their backyards and filled them with oxygen masks, food, and water.

These suspicions turned out to be correct. In February 1950, just days before Senator McCarthy's infamous speech in Wheeling, Klaus Fuchs, a German-born physicist, was arrested in England. Fuchs confessed to spying for the Soviets while working on the Manhattan Project—the top-secret U.S. program to develop the atomic bomb during World War II.

Fuchs' arrest and confession uncovered a spy ring that had passed atomic secrets to the Soviets during World War II. This ring included a man named Julius Rosenberg and his wife, Ethel.

Klaus Fuchs passed valuable atomic secrets to the Soviets during and after World War II.

A member of the spy ring, David Greenglass, testified that Ethel, his sister, had typed notes that contained nuclear secrets, which were passed along to Soviet agents.

The Rosenbergs were arrested shortly after the outbreak of the Korean War. By the time of their trial in March 1951, U.S. troops in Korea were facing a much bigger force made up of soldiers from communist China. Thousands of Americans had died, and there seemed to be no end in sight. There could not have been a worse time to be labeled a communist spy in the United States.

U.S. troops in Korea not only battled communist forces but also fought to survive below-zero temperatures.

The Rosenberg trial lasted just two weeks. They were both convicted and sentenced to death. The judge in the case, Irving Kaufman, went so far as to blame the couple for the war in Korea:

> *I believe your conduct in putting into the hands of the Russians the A-bomb ... has already caused, in my opinion, the Communist aggression in Korea, with the resultant casualties exceeding 50,000 and who knows but that millions more of innocent people may pay the price for your treason.*

The Rosenberg decision greatly divided Americans. Many argued that it was impossible for them to receive a fair trial at the height of the Red Scare. Others claimed that even if the Rosenbergs were guilty, their offense did not warrant the death penalty. Fuchs, who had shared much more vital information, was sentenced to only 14 years in prison. Nevertheless, after several appeals, the Rosenbergs were executed in June 1953.

The Rosenberg case is still debated today. Decoded top-secret messages have since shown that Julius passed secrets to the Soviets. In fact, a Soviet agent claimed to have met with him 50 times, but he said that Rosenberg never provided vital information. Neither of these sources mentioned Ethel Rosenberg.

Concerns about atomic security reached beyond the Rosenbergs. Robert Oppenheimer, who had

directed the Manhattan Project, also came under fire. After World War II, he was hailed as the father of the atomic bomb, who had helped defeat Japan. But Oppenheimer's ideas about atomic weapons shifted after he saw the

Ethel and Julius Rosenberg were the only U.S. civilians executed for espionage during the Cold War.

55

Across the United States, crowds staged protests to try to save the Rosenbergs from execution.

destruction they caused. Later, as head of the Atomic Energy Commission, he argued against an arms race with the Soviets. He was also opposed to the new plans to develop a hydrogen bomb. Politicians

and other scientists questioned Oppenheimer's motives. They worried he was trying to help the Soviets by slowing down America's development of nuclear weapons.

High-level government officials accused Oppenheimer of working with communists during the 1930s. He was called to answer the charges before the Atomic Energy Commission. His brother had admitted to HUAC that he was a communist, as did a number of Oppenheimer's students who also had worked on the Manhattan Project. Though the FBI had been watching him closely for years, no evidence of Oppenheimer's disloyalty was found. Despite this testimony, the Atomic Energy Commission still decided that Oppenheimer was a security risk.

Oppenheimer lost his security clearance and was removed from the commission, which was a huge blow to his reputation.

Americans from many different professions, not just within the government, also came under attack. People feared that pro-communist teachers

THE VENONA PROJECT

The Venona Project was a top secret U.S. Army system that decoded Soviet intelligence messages during World War II. It was so secret that President Truman hadn't even known about it. The Venona materials were not released to the public until 1995. The findings proved that there were many spies working in the U.S. government, including Julius Rosenberg and possibly Alger Hiss. Much of the government's doubt about spies during the McCarthy era could have been avoided if the president had been aware of Venona.

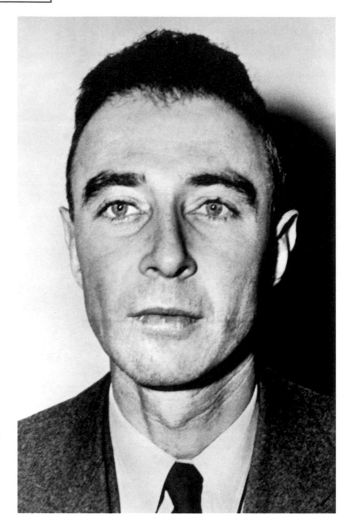

Robert Oppenheimer's call to limit the production of nuclear weapons led to suspicions that he sympathized with the Soviets.

were corrupting the minds of America's young people. More than 100 college professors alone lost their jobs this way. Many others quit because they believed loyalty oaths violated their right to free speech.

During the Red Scare, anyone whose beliefs strayed from the majority was a suspect. People who fought for racial equality were called communists, as were people who wanted to limit the development of nuclear weapons.

Employees who had been cleared by loyalty boards were checked again and were often found guilty without any new evidence. Many of the accused attempted to protect themselves by invoking the Fifth Amendment. This section of the Bill of Rights states that a person can refuse to be a witness against himself or herself at a hearing or trial. For many, pleading the fifth, as it was called, led others to assume they were trying to hide their guilt. Many of the people who exercised their constitutional right were branded Fifth Amendment communists and were dismissed from their jobs. It seemed that nothing—not even a person's basic constitutional rights—could protect suspected communists from McCarthyism.

The McCarthy Committee

Chapter

6

McCarthy's anticommunism crusade continued to gain steam, and it seemed that
no one was safe from his attacks. In June 1951,
he even took aim at George Marshall, who was
serving one year as U.S. secretary of defense.

In a rambling three-hour speech before
the Senate, McCarthy blamed Marshall for
everything from the attack on Pearl Harbor to
the fall of China. He made the ridiculous charges
that Marshall had worked side-by-side with
Joseph Stalin and was purposely trying to aid the
Soviet Union by weakening the U.S. military. He
suggested that:

> *[Marshall's actions] must be a product of a
> great conspiracy, a conspiracy on a scale so
> immense as to dwarf any previous venture in
> the history of men.*

*McCarthy waged an ongoing anticommunist crusade,
during which he attacked some of America's most prominent
politicians, including George Marshall and President Truman.*

COMMUNIST PARTY ORGANIZATION U.S.

NO. OF COMMUN... ...STS IN U.S.A. UNDER
DISCIPLINE F... ...OW 1950 - 59,174
ESTIMATED N... ...LLOW TRAVELERS
...540,000

...195+
NO. OF ...STS IN U.S.A. UNDER DISCIPLINE
FROM ... ...W 1954 - SLIGHTLY OVER 25,000
ESTI... ...O. OF FELLOW TRAVELERS
... - 1954 - SLIGHTLY OVER 250,000

McCarthy's speech shocked his fellow senators. Marshall had served his country bravely in two world wars and earned worldwide praise for his Marshall Plan. Few could understand McCarthy's motives for trying to smear the name of such an admired and decent man. Even the senator's most loyal supporters could not defend his outrageous actions.

Among those infuriated by this assault on Marshall's character was Dwight D. Eisenhower, a Republican candidate for president. Few Americans were as beloved as Eisenhower, who had commanded Allied forces in Europe during World War II. He considered Marshall his close friend and mentor. Eisenhower wanted to speak out against McCarthy's claims on the campaign trail, but his political advisers convinced him to keep quiet. They worried that attacking the popular senator might hurt Eisenhower's chances of getting elected.

This type of thinking was typical of the time. Many politicians were afraid to tangle with McCarthy out of fear that they would become his next target.

Eisenhower was elected president in November 1952, with Richard Nixon as his vice president. McCarthy won reelection. With a fellow Republican in the White House, many assumed McCarthy would back off his anticommunist campaign. They were wrong.

Dwight Eisenhower (right) and running mate Richard Nixon (holding child) were elected in a landslide victory over their Democratic challengers in November 1952.

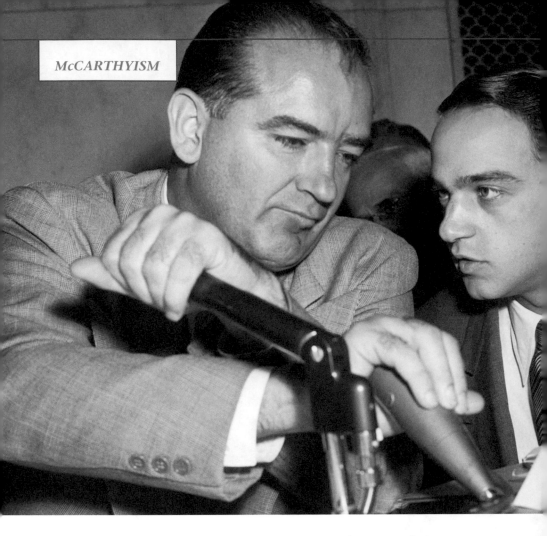

In January 1953, McCarthy became chairman of the Government Operations Committee, considered to be one of the least important Senate committees. In fact, one of his closest allies, Senator Bob Taft of Ohio, told a reporter:

We've got McCarthy where he can't do any harm.

But McCarthy had other ideas. As head of the Permanent Investigations Subcommittee, he planned to step up his search for communists in the government.

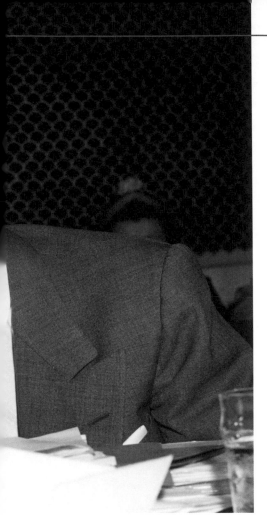

Roy Cohn (right) was Joseph McCarthy's closest adviser during the years he chaired the Permanent Investigations Subcommittee.

McCarthy assembled a committee that included three Republican and three Democratic senators. He also hired a fiery young lawyer named Roy Cohn as his chief legal counsel.

The 26-year-old Cohn had worked on several major anticommunism court cases, including the Rosenberg case. Cohn convinced McCarthy to hire his friend David Schine, the son of a millionaire hotel and restaurant owner. Though he was not a lawyer, Schine was brought on as an unpaid consultant.

65

McCarthy's first high-profile investigation targeted the Voice of America (VOA). This area of the State Department delivered radio programming around the world in nearly 50 languages. McCarthy hoped to uncover a communist plot to alter the pro-American message of the broadcasts.

The image we have today of McCarthy as a loud, bullying interrogator began during the televised VOA hearings. TV viewers got to watch VOA employees accuse their co-workers and bosses of disloyalty. One witness committed suicide on the day he was scheduled to testify. The hearings seemed to produce the intended effect. Within a couple of months, more than 800 VOA employees were dismissed.

Next, McCarthy's committee went after State Department libraries located in foreign countries. Cohn convinced McCarthy to send him and Schine on a fact-finding tour in April 1953 that took them to several major European cities. The pair searched library shelves and card catalogs for books with pro-communist messages. The European press saw them as a couple of young bullies who had been given too much power.

McCarthy's researchers compiled a list of 30,000 books they considered to be anti-American. Overseas libraries were forced to remove these suspect books from their shelves. These included books by Whittaker Chambers and Dashiell

Hammett, a former communist who wrote the detective classic *The Maltese Falcon*. At the time, reports even circulated that fearful librarians were burning books.

A trip McCarthy's assistants David Schine (left) and Roy Cohn took to Europe became a major embarrassment for the senator.

President Eisenhower spoke out against book burning. He told a crowd at Dartmouth College:

> *Don't be afraid to go in your library and read every book as long as any document does not offend our own ideas of decency.*

But he refused to directly criticize McCarthy. He despised the way McCarthy bashed opponents in the press and did not want to resort to the same tactics. Eisenhower privately told his advisers:

> *I just will not—I refuse—to get down in the gutter with that guy.*

McCarthy next turned his attention to the U.S. Army. He had received a tip about communist activity at Fort Monmouth, New Jersey, which had a top-secret research center for developing weapons and radar systems.

Working from information passed to him by the base commander, McCarthy hoped to uncover a major spy ring. He also wanted to link Fort Monmouth employees with Julius Rosenberg, who had worked at the base in the early 1940s.

WEDDING BELLS

On September 29, 1953, McCarthy married his assistant, Jean Kerr. A crowd of more than 900 people attended the ceremony, including future U.S. presidents John F. Kennedy and Richard Nixon. The newlyweds cut short their planned three-week honeymoon after McCarthy learned of suspected communists at Fort Monmouth.

The Democrats on his committee were absent for most of the Fort Monmouth hearings. They were boycotting the committee in protest of the chairman's methods. This meant that McCarthy was free to conduct his hearings however he saw fit. The Fort Monmouth hearings lasted for six months and included more than 30 witnesses. But in the end, the investigation failed to turn up any spies.

Senator Joseph McCarthy (right) battled against Robert T. Stevens, secretary of the U.S. Army, during the Fort Monmouth hearings.

69

McCarthy's next Army case involved Irving Peress, a dentist who had been drafted in October 1952. When filling out his loyalty questionnaire, Peress avoided answering questions about his political views. The case was not properly reviewed until a year later, when Peress was deemed a security risk. But less than a week after the report was issued, he was promoted to major. After Army officials realized their mistake, Peress received an honorable discharge.

McCarthy wanted to know who exactly had promoted Peress, as well as the names of the officers who had handled the dentist's case. McCarthy wanted answers, but he did not get them from Peress. The dentist repeatedly pleaded the fifth when he appeared before the committee in January 1954. McCarthy then focused on finding out what had gone wrong in the Army investigation. In February 1954, Peress' commanding officer, General Ralph W. Zwicker, appeared before the committee.

When the general refused to answer questions about Peress' promotion, the senator launched a vicious attack against him. McCarthy compared Zwicker to someone with "the brains of a five-year-old." He then said that the general was "not fit to wear that uniform."

This time, McCarthy had finally gone too far. In an effort to bring down a dentist, McCarthy had smeared a decorated World War II hero who

was also a friend of the president's. Army officials and Eisenhower had finally had enough of Joseph McCarthy and his grandstanding hearings that seemed to accomplish nothing. McCarthy's attack on Zwicker marked the beginning of the end for the senator.

McCarthy's attack on General Ralph W. Zwicker would lead to the senator's decline.

71

The Fall of McCarthy

Chapter

7

On March 9, 1954, McCarthy's reputation was dealt a serious blow when a revealing report aired on *See It Now,* a popular TV series. The show's host was Edward R. Murrow, the most respected newscaster on television. The half-hour program showed footage of McCarthy at his worst—yelling at witnesses and making claims that Murrow showed to be false. Murrow said:

> *This is no time for men who oppose Senator McCarthy's methods to keep silent. … We cannot defend freedom abroad by deserting it at home. The actions of the junior senator from Wisconsin have caused alarm and dismay amongst our allies abroad and given considerable comfort to our enemies.*

Edward R. Murrow's reports on McCarthy helped change many Americans' feelings toward the senator.

In the 24 hours following the airing of the program, the CBS television network received more than 12,000 phone calls. For every one caller who disagreed with the report, 15 were in favor of it.

About a month later, McCarthy appeared on *See It Now* to respond to Murrow's report. Using his usual attack methods, McCarthy claimed the show's esteemed host had once "engaged in propaganda for communist causes." Murrow later summed up the senator's tactics by saying, "Anyone who criticizes or opposes McCarthy's methods must be a communist, and if that be true, there are an awful lot of communists in this country." McCarthy's appearance on the show probably did more to hurt his reputation than repair it. One thing was clear: He was steadily losing support.

McCarthy accused Murrow of belonging to an organization that trained communist spies.

Another event that hastened McCarthy's downfall centered on his aide David Schine, who had been drafted in 1953. On March 11, 1954, the U.S. Army released a report charging McCarthy and Cohn with pressuring Army officers to give special treatment to Schine. Eisenhower's advisers had urged Army officials to release the report following McCarthy's earlier battle with General Zwicker.

The evidence was overwhelming. The 40-page report showed that Schine was given passes to leave the base more than any of the other soldiers. He also received other perks, including permission to leave in the middle of drills to take phone calls. According to the report, Cohn threatened Army officials with more McCarthy committee investigations if they did not cooperate. McCarthy, however, believed that the report was meant to discourage any further investigation of the Army. He told his committee:

> *The Army is holding Schine hostage to get me to lay off.*

The Army-McCarthy hearings began on April 22, 1954. McCarthy's usual role was reversed. Now he was the one who stood accused and had to answer tough questions before his own committee. An attorney from Boston named Joseph Nye Welch was selected to represent the U.S. Army. The 63-year-old Welch was a skilled debater who succeeded in putting McCarthy on the defensive.

At one point, McCarthy produced a letter that warned of security risks at the Fort Monmouth base. McCarthy claimed that FBI Director J. Edgar Hoover wrote the letter. But Welch proved it was an altered copy of the original. The serious content of the letter no longer mattered. Welch had shown that McCarthy had stooped to using false evidence. This seemed to prove the charge by McCarthy's critics that he would do anything for his own gain.

In early June, the hearings reached a boiling point. Fred Fisher, a young lawyer from Welch's firm, had at one time belonged to a group that was suspected of communist ties. Welch knew that McCarthy might make Fisher a target, so he decided to leave Fisher out of the hearings.

But on June 9, as Welch teased Cohn about his failure to discover any real communists, an enraged McCarthy grabbed the microphone. He said that if Welch wanted information about communists, he should know about one who was working in his own law firm. Welch paused to gather himself and said:

Until this moment, Senator, I think I never really gauged your cruelty or your recklessness.

He then explained that Fisher no longer belonged to the suspect organization and had been asked not to work on the McCarthy hearings. Cohn desperately signaled for McCarthy to stop his attack, but the furious senator pressed on.

Welch tried to put a stop to McCarthy's ranting. He famously scolded him by saying:

> *Let us not assassinate this lad any further, Senator. You've done enough. Have you no decency, sir? At long last, have you left no sense of decency?*

The crowd in the hearing room burst into applause for Welch. But McCarthy persisted. He seemed completely unaware of the damage his outburst would do to his reputation.

Joseph Nye Welch (center) and his aides reviewed evidence during the Army-McCarthy hearings.

The growing popularity of television played a major role in destroying McCarthy's career.

The hearings were televised live each day. For the first time, many Americans were able to see McCarthy in action. For weeks, millions of viewers watched him bully witnesses and constantly interrupt other speakers. His behavior seemed to confirm all the bad things his critics had been saying about him. For many, McCarthy's attack on Fred Fisher was the last straw.

78

After two months of hearings, the committee issued two separate reports. The Democrats were critical of McCarthy and Cohn's attempts to gain favors for Schine. The Republicans, on the other hand, claimed there was not enough evidence to prove the duo had done anything wrong. In the end, the committee report did not matter much. The American people had seen the real Senator McCarthy, and they were not impressed.

Cohn resigned his position in late June 1954. On July 30, Senator Ralph Flanders of Vermont asked the U.S. Senate to censure McCarthy. Censure is an official reprimand. It is a serious matter—just one step below being expelled from the Senate. At the time, censure had been used only three times before in the Senate, including one case where two senators got into a fistfight on the Senate floor.

The censure hearings lasted almost three weeks. On December 2, 1954, McCarthy was censured by a vote of 67-22. Although the ruling did not actually take away any of McCarthy's rights or privileges as a senator, it all but destroyed his power. Almost overnight, the press stopped covering him. Nothing he said or did seemed to be newsworthy anymore. Less than three years later, McCarthy would be dead. On May 2, 1957, the senator died after his liver failed, a complication related to alcoholism. He was only 47 years old.

Aftermath and Lessons

Chapter

8

Not long after Joseph McCarthy's fall from power, the McCarthy era also began to wind down. HUAC continued its hunt for communists, but its power began to disappear. Like McCarthy himself, the search for communists no longer made headlines.

By that time, CPUSA was in decline. Membership was down to only a few thousand people. Since the start of the Cold War, undercover FBI agents had been joining the party to break it up from within. Some people joked that the party was mostly made up of FBI agents. One government official said:

I always believed ... that the FBI kept the Communist Party alive through the dues payments of their agents.

In the late 1950s, the Supreme Court of the United States questioned the interrogation methods used by the authorities in seeking to uncover communists.

Late in the 1950s, the U.S. Supreme Court over-turned some of the unfair laws that had been passed during the Red Scare. The court declared that people could not be dismissed from jobs for refusing to answer questions about their political beliefs. This upheld a person's right to exercise the Fifth Amendment. The court also ruled that people suspected of disloyalty should be able to see secret files about themselves.

On Monday June 17, 1957, the Supreme Court struck down three major anticommunist rulings. One of the biggest decisions was *Yates v. United States*. The court's decision in this case challenged the Smith Act, which made it illegal for anyone to belong to a group that wanted to overthrow the government. This act had been used to imprison dozens of CPUSA members. The court cited the important difference between simply stating beliefs and encouraging illegal actions based on those beliefs. Being a member of CPUSA did not mean a person was trying to overthrow the government. More than 81 cases against Communist Party members were dismissed as a part of this ruling.

BLACKLIST LIFTED

In 1957, Robert Rich won an Academy Award for writing a film called *The Brave One*. People at the ceremony wondered, "Who is Robert Rich?" The film was actually written by Dalton Trumbo, one of the blacklisted Hollywood Ten. Using false names was the only way many blacklisted writers could get work. After more than a decade, the blacklist finally was lifted when Trumbo received credit for his work on the film *Exodus* in 1959.

In another ruling that day, *Watkins v. United States*, the court warned against the abuse of power by government committees. HUAC and committees like the one chaired by McCarthy did not have unlimited power to investigate anyone they pleased. The baseless accusations of the McCarthy era would no longer be tolerated.

Critics of the court's decisions referred to June 17 as Red Monday. President Eisenhower even worried that the court had gone too far to protect communists. But for many Americans, the rulings signaled the end of a sad period in U.S. history.

Roy Cohn (left) remained one of Joseph McCarthy's most vocal defenders years after the senator's death.

However, the U.S. Supreme Court decisions gave little comfort to the untold number of Americans who had seen their reputations damaged or careers destroyed.

Today, McCarthyism is used to describe any public accusation of disloyalty without real proof. The term is not just limited to the four years that the Wisconsin senator was in the spotlight. Instead, it refers to the entire post-World War II period when many Americans suffered the loss of their basic freedoms because of a widespread fear of what was called a red menace.

The subject of Joseph McCarthy continues to divide America. Many of his supporters at the time shared the opinion of the senator's friend and employee Roy Cohn, who explained:

> *McCarthy used the best methods available to him to fight a battle that needed to be fought. The methods were far from perfect, but they were not nearly as imperfect as uninformed critics suggest. ... He may have been wrong in his details, but he was right in his essentials.*

Recent evidence has shown that McCarthy's basic claim was true. Many communists did work in the State Department and in other areas of government in the 1940s. However, most communist spies had already been caught or had left the government by the time McCarthy started his crusade. For all the hysteria he drummed up, McCarthy turned up little information that was not already in the

FBI's files. His critics have argued that he proved to be more dangerous to America than any of the people he attacked.

There is little chance of another Red Scare in America. The collapse of the Soviet Union in the early 1990s brought an end to the Cold War. But this does not guarantee that the United States is free from the fear and mistrust that led to the rise of McCarthyism.

During times of war and national crisis, fear is at its highest, and individual freedoms often suffer as a result. As the United States learned during the McCarthy era, if we don't fight to defend the basic rights we cherish, they might end up being taken away from us.

A red flag was the symbol of the Soviet Union after the Revolution of 1917, but after the collapse of the empire in 1991, a new white, blue, and red flag was chosen to symbolize Russia.

85

Timeline

November 14, 1908

Joseph McCarthy is born in Grand Chute, Wisconsin

November 1917

Bolsheviks rise to power in Russia

February 6, 1919

More than 65,000 Seattle, Washington, union workers go on strike in what is the first general strike in U.S. history

June 2, 1919

Bomb explodes outside the home of U.S. Attorney General A. Mitchell Palmer

September 1919

Two separate communist parties form in the United States

November 7, 1919

J. Edgar Hoover leads nationwide raids against suspected radicals

January 2, 1920

Palmer Raids round up thousands of suspected communists in more than 30 U.S. cities

October 29, 1929

U.S. stock market crashes, leading to the start of the Great Depression

November 8, 1932

Franklin D. Roosevelt is elected U.S. president; he soon begins fulfilling his campaign promise of a New Deal for America

June 7, 1938

House Un-American Activities Committee (HUAC) is established

September 1, 1939

Germany invades Poland, starting World War II

June 28, 1940

The Smith Act, officially known as the Alien Registration Act, is signed into law

June 22, 1941

Germany invades the Soviet Union

December 7, 1941

Japanese warplanes launch surprise attack on the U.S. naval base in Pearl Harbor, Hawaii; the United States enters World War II the following day

February 1945

Leaders of the United States, the United Kingdom, and the Soviet Union meet in Yalta to discuss plans for postwar Europe

August 6, 1945

The United States drops an atomic bomb on Hiroshima, Japan; a second bomb is dropped on Nagasaki, Japan, three days later

November 1946

Joseph McCarthy of Wisconsin is elected to the U.S. Senate

March 22, 1947

President Harry S. Truman issues Executive Order 9835, creating a loyalty program for all federal employees

October 1947

Members of the Hollywood Ten appear before HUAC

April–May 1948

The Hollywood Ten are convicted of contempt of Congress

June 1948–September 1949

Planes deliver food, medicine, and other supplies to the people of West Berlin as part of the Berlin Airlift

August 1948

Whittaker Chambers and Alger Hiss testify before HUAC

December 2, 1948

Chambers leads HUAC investigators to stolen government documents hidden in a pumpkin field

August 1949

The Soviet Union successfully tests its first nuclear bomb

October 1949

Mao Tse-tung declares formation of the People's Republic of China

January 21, 1950

Alger Hiss is convicted of perjury

February 2, 1950

Klaus Fuchs is arrested in Great Britain and charged with sharing atomic secrets with the Soviets

February 9, 1950

Joseph McCarthy tells an audience in Wheeling, West Virginia, that there are 205 known communists working in the State Department

Timeline

March 1, 1950

Klaus Fuchs is sentenced to 14 years in prison

March 8, 1950

The Tydings Committee begins hearings to investigate McCarthy's charge that communists are in the State Department

June 25, 1950

The Korean War begins when communist troops from North Korea launch a surprise invasion of South Korea

July 17, 1950

The FBI arrests Julius Rosenberg on spying charges

April 5, 1951

Ethel and Julius Rosenberg are sentenced to death

November 1, 1952

The United States detonates the first hydrogen bomb

November 4, 1952

Dwight D. Eisenhower is elected U.S. president; Joseph McCarthy is reelected for a second term in the U.S. Senate

January 1953

McCarthy becomes chair of the Senate Government Operations Committee

June 19, 1953

Ethel and Julius Rosenberg are executed

July 27, 1953

The Korean War ends

March 9, 1954

Edward R. Murrow reports on McCarthy on *See It Now*

April 1954

Army–McCarthy hearings begin

June 9, 1954

Joseph Welch asks McCarthy, "Have you no decency?" during televised hearings

June 29, 1954

Atomic Energy Commission removes the security clearance of Robert Oppenheimer

December 2, 1954

The U.S. Senate approves censure of McCarthy by a vote of 67-22

May 2, 1957

Joseph McCarthy dies in Bethesda, Maryland

ON THE WEB

For more information on *McCarthyism*, use FactHound.

1 Go to *www.facthound.com*

2 Type in this book ID: 075652007X

3 Click on the *Fetch It* button. FactHound will find Web sites related to this book.

HISTORIC SITES

Harry S. Truman Presidential Library and Museum
U.S. Highway 24 and Delaware Street
Independence, MO 64050-1798
816/268-8200

Visitors can view exhibits about the Cold War and the Korean War.

Dwight D. Eisenhower Presidential Library and Museum
200 S.E. Fourth St.
Abilene, KS 67410
785/263-4751

Visitors can view exhibits about the Cold War and the Red Scare.

LOOK FOR MORE BOOKS IN THIS SERIES

The Collapse of the Soviet Union:
The End of an Empire
ISBN 0-7565-2009-6

Miranda v. Arizona:
The Rights of the Accused
ISBN 0-7565-2008-8

The Little Rock Nine:
Struggle for Integration
ISBN 0-7565-2011-8

The New Deal:
Rebuilding America
ISBN 0-7565-2096-7

McCarthyism:
The Red Scare
ISBN 0-7565-2007-X

Watergate:
Scandal in the White House
ISBN 0-7565-2010-X

A complete list of **Snapshots in History** titles is available on our Web site: *www.compasspointbooks.com*

Glossary

accusation
a charge against a person for doing
something wrong

aggression
the act of launching an attack or invasion

amendment
a change made to a law or legal document

bail
money required for the release of an
arrested person until he or she is tried
in court

capitalism
an economic system in which the
means of production (such as factories,
materials, and tools) are privately owned
and operated. The United States uses the
capitalist system

communism
a belief system based on government
ownership of all land and industry

conservative
a person who favors traditional values
and supports limited government
involvement in people's lives

contempt
to show disrespect to the authority of a
court of law

deport
to expel a foreigner from a country

hysteria
fear or panic

integration
bringing people of different races
together; the opposite of segregation

interrogator
a person who questions others, usually in
an official role

investigation
the process of collecting evidence to
determine if a crime has been committed

labor unions
organizations formed by workers. Unions
fight to improve wages and working
conditions for their members.

microfilm
a small roll of film that stores information

physicist
a scientist who studies matter and energy

politician
a person who holds a public office

prosecute
to carry out a legal action against a person
accused of a crime

radicals
people who are extreme in their thoughts
or behavior

Source Notes

Chapter 1

Page 10, line 10: Edwin R. Bayley. *Joe McCarthy and the Press*. Madison: University of Wisconsin Press, 1981, pp. 17–18.

Chapter 2

Page 26, line 16: Ted Morgan. *Reds: McCarthyism in Twentieth-Century America*. New York: Random House, 2003, p. 209.

Chapter 3

Page 34, line 30: Arthur Herman. *Joseph McCarthy: Reexamining the Life and Legacy of America's Most Hated Senator*. New York: Free Press, 2000, p. 108.

Chapter 4

Page 43, line 23: Ellen Schrecker. *Many Are the Crimes: McCarthyism in America*. Boston: Little, Brown, 1998, p. 243.

Page 46, line 6: "Stand or Fall." *Time*. 3 April, 1950.

Page 48, line 4: "Silly Numbers Game." *Time*. 15 May, 1950.

Chapter 5

Page 54, line 5: "Text of Judge Kaufman's Statement on Sentencing Bomb Spies." *The New York Times*. 6 April, 1951, p. 10.

Chapter 6

Page 60, line 14: *Major Speeches and Debates of Senator Joe McCarthy, Delivered in the U.S. Senate 1950–1951*. Washington, D.C.: U.S. Government Printing Office, 1953.

Page 64, line 6: Richard Halworth Rovere. *Senator Joe McCarthy*. New York: Harcourt Brace, 1959, p. 188.

Page 68, line 3: "The Texts of Eisenhower Speeches at Dartmouth and Oyster Bay." *The New York Times*. 15 June, 1953, p. 10.

Page 68, line 10: Emmett John Hughes. *The Ordeal of Power: A Political Memoir of the Eisenhower Years*. New York: Atheneum, 1963, p. 92.

Source Notes

Page 70, line 25: *Reds: McCarthyism in Twentieth Century America,* p. 209.

Chapter 7

Page 72, line 10: "The McCarthy Years." *Good Night and Good Luck: The Edward R. Murrow Television Collection.* CBS Inc. 1991.

Page 74, line 8, 10: Ibid.

Page 75, line 20: "The Oak & Ivy." *Time.* 8 March 1954.

Page 76, line 23: "Excerpts from 30th Day of Testimony in Senate Hearings on Army-McCarthy Dispute." *The New York Times.* 10 June 1954, p. 15.

Page 77, line 3: Ibid.

Chapter 8

Page 80, line 14: Frances Stonor Saunders. *The Cultural Cold War: The CIA and the World of Arts and Letters.* New York: New Press, 2000, p. 191.

Page 84, line 17: William K. Klingaman. *Encyclopedia of the McCarthy Era.* New York: Facts on File, 1996, p. 78.

SELECT BIBLIOGRAPHY

Bayley, Edwin R. *Joe McCarthy and the Press*. Madison: University of Wisconsin Press, 1981.

Feuerlicht, Roberta Strauss. *America's Reign of Terror: World War I, the Red Scare, and the Palmer Raids*. New York: Random House, 1971.

Fried, Richard M. *Nightmare in Red: The McCarthy Era in Perspective*. New York: Oxford University Press, 1990.

Herman, Arthur. *Joseph McCarthy: Reexamining the Life and Legacy of America's Most Hated Senator*. New York: Free Press, 2000.

Klingaman, William K. *Encyclopedia of the McCarthy Era*. New York: Facts on File, 1996.

Morgan, Ted. *Reds: McCarthyism in Twentieth-Century America*. New York: Random House, 2003.

Rovere, Richard Halworth. *Senator Joe McCarthy*. New York: Harcourt Brace. 1959.

Saunders, Frances Stonor. *The Cultural Cold War: The CIA and the World of Arts and Letters*. New York: New Press, 2000.

Schrecker, Ellen. *Many Are the Crimes: McCarthyism in America*. Boston: Little, Brown, 1998.

FURTHER READING

Anderson, Dale. *The Making of America: The Cold War Years*. Austin, Texas: Raintree Steck-Vaughn Publishers, 2001.

Notorious Americans and Their Times: Joseph McCarthy and the Cold War. Woodbridge, Conn.: Blackbirch Press, Inc., 1999.

Wroble, Lisa. *The New Deal and the Great Depression in American History*. Berkeley Heights, N.J.: Enslow Publishers, 2002.

Index

A

Acheson, Dean, 11, 35, 43
Army-McCarthy hearings, 75–79
Atomic Energy Commission (AEC), 56, 57
atomic weapons, 30, 50, 51, 52, 54–56, 59

B

Berlin Airlift, 32–33
Berlin, Germany, 28, 32–33
Bill of Rights, 13, 14, 59
blacklisting, 36, 82
Bolsheviks, 16, 20–21
bomb shelters, 51
Budenz, Louis, 46–47

C

capitalism, 24
Chambers, Whittaker, 34, 36, 66
Chiang Kai-shek, 46
China, 10, 46, 53, 60
Churchill, Winston, 28, 29
Cohn, Roy, 65, 66, 75, 76, 79, 84
Cold War, 30, 32, 80
communism, 8–9, 10, 11, 13, 14, 16, 18, 19, 20, 21, 22, 24, 26, 30–31, 33, 34, 37, 42, 49, 80, 82
Communist Party of America, 21
Communist Party of the United States (CPUSA), 20, 24, 26, 34, 80
Constitution of the United States, 13, 14
containment strategy, 30

D

Dartmouth College, 68
Democratic Party, 24, 39, 43, 45, 65, 69, 79
Dies, Martin, 26
duck-and-cover drills, 51

E

Eisenhower, Dwight, 62, 68, 71, 75, 83
espionage. *See* spies.
European Recovery Act, 30–31, 62
Executive Order 9835, 33–34

F

Federal Bureau of Investigation (FBI), 46, 57, 76, 80, 84–85
Fifth Amendment, 59, 82
First Amendment, 14, 36

Fisher, Fred, 76, 78
Flanders, Ralph, 79
Ford, James, 24
Fort Monmouth, New Jersey, 68, 76
Fuchs, Klaus, 52, 54

G

General Intelligence Division, 20
Germany, 26, 27, 28, 29, 32–33
Government Operations Committee (GOC), 64
Grand Chute, Wisconsin, 38
Great Britain, 28, 32
Great Depression, 22, 24–25
Greenglass, David, 53

H

Hammett, Dashiell, 66–67
Hiroshima, Japan, 30, 50
Hiss, Alger, 34–36, 36–37, 44, 57
Hollywood, California, 36, 82
Hoover, J. Edgar, 20, 46, 76
HUAC. *See* Special House Committee on Un-American Activities.
hydrogen bomb, 51, 56

J

Justice Department, 20

K

Kaufman, Irving, 54
Kennedy, John F., 68
Korean War, 49, 53, 54

L

labor strikes, 19, 24, 27
Lattimore, Owen, 46, 47
Lucas, Scott, 48

M

Manhattan Project, 52, 55, 57
Mao Tse-tung, 46
Marquette University, 39
Marshall, George, 30, 60, 62
Marshall Plan, 30–31, 62
McCarthy, Jean Kerr, 68
McCarthy, Joseph
  Army-McCarthy hearings, 75–79
  censure of, 79
  childhood of, 38

as circuit judge, 40
communist list, 10, 42–43
death of, 79
education of, 38–39
Fort Monmouth hearings, 68–69
as Government Operations Committee
    (GOC) chairman, 64
marriage of, 68
Marshall speech, 60, 62
military career, 40, 41
as Permanent Investigations
    Subcommittee chairman, 64–65, 66,
    68–69, 70–71, 75
public support for, 49, 62, 74, 84
on *See It Now* (television program), 74
as senator, 41, 44, 60, 62, 64, 79
speaking tour, 8, 10, 13, 37, 41–42, 42–43
Tydings Committee and, 45–49
Voice of America (VOA) hearings, 66
Murrow, Edward R., 72

N

Nagasaki, Japan, 30, 50
New Deal, 24–25, 26, 39
Nixon, Richard, 36, 49, 62, 68
North Korea, 49
nuclear weapons, 30, 50, 51, 52, 56, 59

O

Oppenheimer, Robert, 54–58

P

Palmer, A. Mitchell, 20
Palmer Raids, 22
Pearl Harbor, Hawaii, 40, 60
Pearson, Drew, 49
Peress, Irving, 70
Permanent Investigations Subcommittee,
    64–65, 66, 68–69, 70–71, 75
Poland, 29, 30
"pumpkin papers," 36

R

radicals, 19, 20
"Red Monday," 83
Red Scare, 13, 22, 46, 50, 54, 58, 82, 85
Republican Party, 8, 25, 26, 33, 40, 43, 44,
    62, 65, 79

Rich, Robert, 82
Roosevelt, Franklin Delano, 24–25, 28, 29,
    30, 39
Rosenberg, Ethel, 52, 53, 54
Rosenberg, Julius, 52, 54, 57, 68
Russia, 16–17, 20, 21

S

Schine, David, 65, 66, 75, 79
See It Now (television program), 72, 74
Senate, 8, 41, 44, 45, 60, 62, 64, 79
Smith Act, 34, 82
South Korea, 49
Soviet Union, 8–9, 13, 16, 20, 26, 27, 28, 29,
    30, 33, 43, 50, 54, 56, 57, 85
Special House Committee on Un-American
    Activities (HUAC), 26, 34, 35, 36, 57,
    80, 83
spies, 10, 20, 33, 34, 47, 50, 52–53, 57, 84
Stalin, Joseph, 28, 30, 60
State Department, 10, 34, 36, 42,
    43, 46, 66, 84

T

Taft, Bob, 64
Truman, Harry, 11, 30, 33, 34, 35, 43, 44,
    51, 57
Trumbo, Dalton, 82
Tydings Committee, 45–49
Tydings, Millard, 45

U

U.S. Army, 68, 70, 75
U.S. Supreme Court, 82–84

V

Venona Project, 57
Voice of America (VOA), 66

W

Watkins v. United States, 83
Welch, Joseph Nye, 75
Wheeling, West Virginia, 8, 37
World War II, 26–27, 28, 50, 52, 55, 57, 62

Y

Yalta Conference, 28, 30, 34
Yates v. United States, 82

Z

Zwicker, Ralph, 70–71, 75

ABOUT THE AUTHOR

Brian Fitzgerald has worked in children's publishing for more than a decade. During that time, he has written about many of the key people and most important events in American history and popular culture—from World War II to Jimi Hendrix. He lives in Stamford, Connecticut.

IMAGE CREDITS